Junior High Bible Study Series

Becoming a Christian

Loveland, Colorado

Group's R.E.A.L. Guarantee to you:

This Group resource incorporates our R.E.A.L. approach to ministry—one that encourages long-term retention and life transformation. It's ministry that's:

Relational
  Because learner-to-learner interaction enhances learning and builds Christian friendships.
Experiential
  Because what learners experience through discussion and action sticks with them up to 9 times longer than what they simply hear or read.
Applicable
  Because the aim of Christian education is to equip learners to be both hearers and doers of God's Word.
Learner-based
  Because learners understand and retain more when the learning process takes into consideration how they learn best.

Becoming a Christian

Junior High Bible Study Series

Copyright © 2003 Group Publishing, Inc.

All rights reserved. No part of this book may be reproduced in any manner whatsoever without prior written permission from the publisher, except where noted in the text and in the case of brief quotations embodied in critical articles and reviews. For information, write Permissions, Group Publishing, Inc., Dept. PD, P.O. Box 481, Loveland, CO 80539.

Visit our Web site: **www.grouppublishing.com**

Credits
Authors: Erin McKay, Pamela J. Shoup, Michael D. Warden, and Jennifer Root Wilger
Editor: Kelli B. Trujillo
Creative Development Editor: Amy Simpson
Chief Creative Officer: Joani Schultz
Copy Editor: Lyndsay E. Gerwing
Art Director: Sharon Anderson
Cover Art Director/Designer: Jeff A. Storm
Cover Photographer: Daniel Treat
Print Production Artist: Tracy K. Donaldson
Production Manager: DeAnne Lear

Unless otherwise noted, Scriptures taken from the HOLY BIBLE, NEW INTERNATIONAL VERSION®. Copyright © 1973, 1978, 1984 by International Bible Society. Used by permission of Zondervan Publishing House. All rights reserved.

ISBN 0-7644-2460-2
10 9 8 7 6 5 4 3 2 1   12 11 10 09 08 07 06 05 04 03

Printed in the United States of America.

Table of Contents

5 • Introduction

9 • Study 1: Missing the Mark
  The Point: Sin separates us from God.
  Scripture Source: Isaiah 59:1-2   Romans 3:23; 6:23
  Ephesians 2:3-5, 8-9

17 • Study 2: A Little Too Cool
  The Point: Pride stops the flow of forgiveness.
  Scripture Source: 2 Kings 5:1-17   Proverbs 3:34

27 • Study 3: The Case of the Empty Tomb
  The Point: Jesus rose from the dead so we can be forgiven.
  Scripture Source: Psalm 49:15   Isaiah 53:12
  John 11:25   Romans 6:23; 10:9-13
  various Gospel passages

37 • Study 4: Face the Light
  The Point: Admitting you're wrong helps you experience God's forgiveness.
  Scripture Source: Psalm 103:8-12   Isaiah 1:18; 53:4-6
  Mark 2:17   Luke 15:8-10
  Romans 4:25–5:1   2 Corinthians 7:10-11
  Hebrews 4:13   1 John 1:8-10

47 • Changed 4 Life

Becoming a Christian

Through this book, teenagers will develop an understanding of what it means to become a Christian and begin a faith relationship with Jesus Christ.

What makes someone a Christian? Attending church regularly? Living in a "Christian" country? Being a generally good person? Celebrating holidays like Christmas or Easter? Giving money to a local church? Wearing a W.W.J.D. bracelet?

The truth is that none of these things make someone a Christian.

Though there are many different Christian denominations in the world with various beliefs and practices, one central belief is common to them all: the basic truth that becoming a Christian means putting one's faith in Jesus Christ and asking for and receiving God's forgiveness for sins. Through this book, teenagers will develop an understanding of what it means to become a Christian and begin a faith relationship with Jesus Christ.

In the first study, they'll learn that all people are sinful and that sin separates them from God. They'll reflect on how their own sin has affected their relationship with God.

Next, your students will discover that God offers a cure for the problem of sin: forgiveness. They'll consider how pride can often get in the way, preventing people from recognizing their real need for God's forgiveness.

In the third study, teenagers will investigate the biblical account of Jesus' death and resurrection. They'll learn that Jesus paid the penalty for their sins on the cross and that, through faith in him, they can receive God's forgiveness and eternal life.

The last study will help students learn that, by truly repenting of sin, they can experience God's forgiveness and have a new start.

When your teenagers understand what it means to become a Christian, they'll be prepared to experience God's amazing grace and begin growing in a life-changing relationship with him.

Junior high bible study series
About Faith 4 Life

Use Faith 4 Life studies to show your teenagers how the Bible is relevant to their lives. Help them see that God can invade every area of their lives and change them in ways they can only imagine. Encourage your students to go deeper into faith—faith that will sustain them for life! Faith 4 Life forever!

Faith 4 Life: Junior High Bible Study Series helps young teenagers take a Bible-based approach to faith and life issues. Each book in the series contains these important elements:

■ **Life application of Bible truth**—Faith 4 Life studies help teenagers understand what the Bible says and then apply that truth to their lives.

■ **A relevant topic**—Each Faith 4 Life book focuses on one main topic, with four studies to give your students a thorough understanding of how the Bible relates to that topic. These topics were chosen by youth leaders as the ones most relevant for junior high–age students.

■ **One point**—Each study makes one point, centering on that one theme to make sure students really understand the important truth it conveys. This point is stated upfront and throughout the study.

■ **Simplicity**—The studies are easy to use. Each contains a "Before the Study" box that outlines any advance preparation required. Each study also contains a "Study at a Glance" chart so that you can quickly and easily see what supplies you'll need and what each study will involve.

■ **Action and interaction**—Each study relies on experiential learning to help students learn what God's Word has to say. Teenagers discuss and debrief their experiences in large groups, small groups, and individual reflection.

■ **Reproducible handouts**—Faith 4 Life books include reproducible handouts for students. No need for student books!

■ **Tips, tips, and more tips**—Faith 4 Life studies are full of "FYI" tips for the teacher, providing extra ideas, insights into young people, and hints for making the studies go smoothly.

■ **Flexibility**—Faith 4 Life studies include optional activities and bonus activities. Use a study as it's written, or use these options to create the study that works best for your group.

■ **Follow-up ideas**—At the end of each book, you'll find a section called "Changed 4 Life." This section provides ideas for following up with your students to make sure the studies stick with them.

Missing the Mark

Sin. The word itself can weigh anyone down. The judge pounds the gavel and proclaims the verdict—guilty. And it's off to prison—the prison of the mind where guilt relentlessly haunts and accuses. It's a prison we've all experienced. All humans are under the same sentence—we all fall short of the mark.

Some teenagers are intimately acquainted with the concept of sin; they drink, they lie, they steal. Other students may take their sin lightly—after all, it was only gossip or a selfish thought…nothing *big*. What both of these groups of students need to realize is that their sin separates them from the holy, perfect God.

This study explores the way sin affects our relationships with God and will help students discover that freedom from sin comes only through God's grace.

The Point

▶ Sin separates us from God.

Scripture Source

Isaiah 59:1-2
This passage explains that sin separates people from God.

Romans 3:23
Paul explains that all people have sinned.

Romans 6:23
Paul explains that freedom from sin can be found in Jesus.

Ephesians 2:3-5, 8-9
Paul explains that forgiveness for sin is not a result of good works.

The Study at a Glance

Warm-Up (10-15 minutes)

Bull's-Eye!
What students will do: Try to hit a bull's-eye and discuss how the game relates to sin.

Needs: ❑ Bibles ❑ pens
❑ large target ❑ blindfold
❑ masking tape

Bonus Activity (10-15 minutes)

What students will do: Create a "heart monitor" to indicate how guilty they would feel if caught in certain situations and discuss the consequences of sin and guilt.

Needs: ❑ index cards ❑ pencils

Bible Connection (30-40 minutes)

Guilt Trip
What students will do: Travel throughout the room and creatively consider how sin separates them from God through writing letters on their hands and attempting to make "good works" machines.

Needs: ❑ Bibles ❑ marbles
❑ sandwich bags ❑ string
❑ masking tape ❑ poster board
❑ water-soluble marker

Life Application (5-10 minutes)

Wipe It Out
What students will do: Symbolically remove each other's sin objects and letters.

Needs: ❑ Bibles ❑ clean rags
❑ bowl of soapy water

Before the Study →

Before the study, create a large target using markers and newsprint, or purchase a paper target from an outdoor sporting goods store. Hang the target on a wall in your meeting room. Designate a different wall of your meeting room for each station used in this study. Teenagers will "travel" around your room as they go on their "guilt trip." Set out water-soluble markers at Station 1; marbles, sandwich bags, string, masking tape, and sheets of poster board at Station 2; and a bowl of soapy water and clean rags at Station 3.

Warm-Up

Bull's-Eye!
(10 to 15 minutes)

When everyone has arrived, give each student a small piece of masking tape and a pen, then ask students to write their names on their pieces of tape. Explain that they are going to play a game similar to Pin the Tail on the Donkey, but they'll be using the bull's-eye on the wall as their target. Have teenagers take turns blindfolding each other, spinning around, and then trying to stick their pieces of masking tape on the center of the bull's-eye.

When everyone has played, congratulate those students who got the closest to the center.

ASK:

- What are some of the bull's-eyes we aim for in life?
- How often do we "hit" the bull's-eye in those areas? How often do we miss?
- Most people aim for the bull's-eye of being a "good person." Can anyone ever truly hit that bull's-eye and live up to that expectation? Defend your answer.
- What are some examples of ways people miss that bull's-eye?
- How is missing the bull's-eye like sin?

Invite a student to read Romans 3:23. Ask a few volunteers to explain the meaning of the verse in their own words.

SAY:

- In this game we all aimed for the bull's-eye, but many of us missed it. As we look at the target, there is a distance

FYI Use all four Bible studies in this book in sequential order to help your students understand what it truly means to make a faith commitment to Jesus.

FYI Get involved in the action! It's always a good idea to participate in games instead of standing on the sidelines. By participating in this bull's-eye activity, you'll help illustrate that everyone, including *you*, misses the mark in life.

between our markers and the center. In life, we also miss the mark. We fall short of the life God desires for us. Our <u>sin separates us from God.</u>

◀ **The Point**

* Bonus Activity *

(10 to 15 minutes)

If you have time, try this activity after "Bull's-Eye!"

SAY:

■ **Sin and guilt make us respond in funny ways. When we feel guilty, our behavior changes. We treat people differently; we avoid them or try to make up for what we've done.**

Give each student an index card and a pencil.

SAY:

■ **On your card, write one memory of a sinful thought or action that still makes you feel guilty. For example, you might feel guilty because you lied to your mom when you were five or because you said something mean to a friend. Write it down, but do *not* write your name on the card.**

When teenagers have finished, collect the cards.

SAY:

■ **When we sin, we often feel guilty. We feel our hearts pounding faster, especially if we think someone's going to find out what we did. We try to cover up our actions. We try to hide our sin from others. We're now going to create a "heart monitor" to determine how guilty we would feel about different situations.**

Designate one corner of the room as "racing-heart corner" and the opposite corner as "resting-heart corner."

SAY:

■ **I'm going to read some of your cards. As I read each situation, move to the appropriate place in the room to indicate how guilty you would feel about this situation. For example, if you'd feel really guilty about a situation, go to the racing-heart corner. If you wouldn't feel guilty at all, go to the resting-heart corner. If you'd feel somewhat guilty, stand somewhere between the two corners.**

Randomly choose three or four cards, then read them aloud one at a time, allowing teenagers to respond to each card by moving to a different place in the room. After you read each card, have teenagers each turn to a partner and explain why they chose to stand where they are.

After the activity,

ASK:
- ■ Do you think there are levels of sins? big terrible sins and small insignificant sins? Defend your answer.
- ■ Do small sins have the same effect on our relationship with God as big sins? Explain.

SAY:
- ■ Our sinful thoughts and actions affect others. When someone does something really terrible, it hurts others. There are different levels of consequences for different sins. However, even the smallest sin is still sin; it still misses the mark. No matter what the sin is, and no matter how guilty or not guilty we feel about it, it still separates us from God.

Bible Connection

Guilt Trip
(30 to 40 minutes)

Explain that students will take a "guilt trip" around the room, stopping at three stations to consider the effects of sin and guilt on their relationships with God. Begin by having teenagers gather in the Station 1 area.

Prompt students to think about the way sins have caused them to feel separated from God. Challenge each student to think of one specific sin from his or her past or present that he or she feels guilty about, such as actions, thoughts, or spoken words. Pass around a water-soluble marker, and invite the students to each use the marker to write a letter on the palm of one of their hands. The letters should represent words that describe the sins they have chosen.

Have everyone line up against the Station 1 wall, then

SAY:

- ■ Look at the letter on your hand. Think of the sin that letter represents.

After a few moments,

SAY:

■ When I call out the letter written on your hand, step forward.

Call out each of the letters of the alphabet one at a time until all of the students have stepped forward. After they've all stepped forward,

SAY:

■ Imagine that you are facing God. Hold your lettered hand in front of your face, palm out. As you do this, think about the situation your letter represents. Think about how that sin has created a barrier between you and God.

Have students form pairs so they can discuss these questions:

■ How would your friendships be affected if you held your hand in front of your face all the time?

■ How is that physical barrier similar to the way your relationship with God is affected by your sin?

■ Describe a time guilt has gotten in the way of a relationship in your life.

Have pairs read Isaiah 59:1-2 and discuss this question:

■ Describe a time you've felt separated from God because of sins or guilt. What did that feel like?

Many teenagers struggle with guilt. Sometimes this guilt is very real and is a consequence of sinful thoughts or actions. However, sometimes it's just false guilt. False guilt is usually fueled by several sources—for example, others' unrealistic expectations, self-imposed perfectionism, or a misplaced sense of responsibility for the world's problems. Teenagers need to learn to recognize false guilt and also to face their true guilt for sins they've committed, such as lying to their parents, cheating on tests, or betraying friends.

As you discuss the topic of guilt with your students, you may want to use this chart to help them distinguish between true and false guilt. ▼

FALSE GUILT	TRUE GUILT
makes teenagers feel bad about themselves.	indicates problems or sins in teenagers' lives that need attention (**John 16:7-8**).
promotes anger and low self-esteem.	promotes "the kind of sorrow God wants" (**2 Corinthians 7:10**).
motivates teenagers to avoid facing their problems.	motivates teenagers to change problem behaviors (**2 Corinthians 7:11**).
leads to isolation.	leads to forgiveness (**1 John 1:9**).

When pairs finish, invite volunteers to tell the group what they discussed. Then

SAY:

- As we move to our next station, think about other sins in your life you've felt guilty about.

After students have moved to the Station 2 wall, invite teenagers to form groups of three, and have trios discuss the following questions:

- What are some ways people try to make up for the sins and guilt in their lives?
- Do you think these actions work? Why or why not?

Have trios read Ephesians 2:3-5, 8-9 and discuss their reactions to it. While trios are talking, set out marbles, sandwich bags, string, masking tape, and poster board.

When groups have finished talking,

SAY:

- We all miss the mark—we all fall short. People throughout history have tried to make up for their failures and sins by doing good things.
- In your trios, create a "machine," using the supplies at this station, that represents the good works people do to try to make up for sin. The marbles you have represent sin. Try to create a machine that represents the ways people try to use good works to get rid of sin. You must stay in your area as you work on your machines. Be prepared to tell the rest of the group how your machine represents good works.

When trios are ready, invite them to demonstrate their machines and explain how they represent good works. Encourage groups to tell what they like about each other's creations. Then

ASK:

- How did it feel to try to create a machine that would get rid of your marbles?
- Did any of the machines really work? Are the marbles really gone, or were they just moved around?
- If you had other supplies, would it be possible to create a machine that actually completely got rid of the marbles so that they no longer existed? Explain.

> **FYI** Some teenagers may want to talk with you one-on-one about sin. Tell teenagers that you're available to talk more with any of them at another time.

- **How were your efforts to create your machine similar to the ways people try to bridge the gap between them and God that is caused by their sin?**

Prompt students to work together in their trios to create necklaces. They should each take a sandwich bag, fill it with marbles, and then use string to tie the bag and hang it around their necks.

When trios finish, have them gather near Station 3.

SAY:

- **Ultimately, our efforts to get rid of sin by our own good deeds get us nowhere—the sin is still there. We're still separated from God. Like the weight of the necklaces you now wear, sin can weigh you down. But there is a way to bridge the gap of separation.**

Wipe It Out
(5 to 10 minutes)

Life Application

Have teenagers form a circle, and invite a student to read Romans 6:23. Ask volunteers to explain the key words in the verse, such as *wages*, *sin*, *death*, *gift*, and *life*.

SAY:

- **The Bible tells us that <u>sin separates us from God</u>, leading to spiritual death—but that isn't the end of the story! Through Jesus, we can accept God's gift of love and forgiveness and develop a life-filled relationship with God!**

◀ **The Point**

Explain that students will physically represent what it is like to accept Jesus' gift of forgiveness of sin. Have students form pairs. Distribute clean rags, and set out the bowl of soapy water. Invite pairs to "wipe out" each other's guilt by washing the letters off their partners' hands. Also, have teenagers remove the marble necklaces from their partners' necks.

When pairs finish, have them pray together, thanking God that he offers forgiveness for sins through Jesus. Conclude by telling students that you are available to discuss sin and the forgiveness offered by Jesus on an individual basis with students who have questions.

FYI If you are planning on covering the remaining three lessons in this book, it would be a good idea at this point to tell students that in the upcoming weeks they'll be studying more about faith in Jesus and God's gift of forgiveness.

A Little Too Cool

Study 2

PRIDE — BETTER

DANGER

Every teenager has something to feel proud about: grades, good looks, athletic accomplishments, friends, family relationships, social status, creative talents, intelligence, musical abilities, or sense of humor, just to name a few. A healthy sense of pride and self-esteem is a good thing! But pride can also be dangerous.

Pride can keep someone from saying, "I'm sorry."

Pride can prompt someone to look down on someone else.

Pride can turn into arrogance.

And most dangerous of all, pride can prevent someone from recognizing and truly repenting of sin. Repentance takes tremendous humility!

In this study, teenagers will compare their reactions to brokenness in their lives with Naaman's reaction to his leprosy and then use Naaman's story to examine the connection between sin, pride, forgiveness, and hope.

By understanding Naaman's experience, teenagers can discover how pride can undermine their ability to recognize their need for God's forgiveness.

The Point

▶ Pride stops the flow of forgiveness.

Scripture Source

2 Kings 5:1-17
Elisha instructs the leper Naaman to wash seven times in the Jordan River so he can be healed.

Proverbs 3:34
Solomon writes about the relationship between pride, humility, and grace.

The Study at a Glance

Warm-Up (20-30 minutes)

Numb-Friends League
What students will do: Form two teams to see which can "numbify" one of its members the best.
Needs:
- ❏ toilet paper
- ❏ tape
- ❏ paper wads
- ❏ newsprint
- ❏ marker
- ❏ "Diagnosis: Leprosy" handouts (p. 25)
- ❏ "Diagnosis: Sin" handouts (p. 25)

Bible Connection (15-20 minutes)

The Price of Pride
What students will do: Learn about Naaman and talk about how Naaman's story can teach them about sin, pride, and forgiveness.
Needs: ❏ Bibles

Bonus Activity (5-10 minutes)

What students will do: Learn about Naaman in 2 Kings 5 by presenting an "act as you go" skit.
Needs:
- ❏ Bibles
- ❏ index cards
- ❏ pen
- ❏ tape or pins

Life Application (up to 10 minutes)

Cleansings
What students will do: Be challenged to wear their "sin" lists until they take private time to talk to God about them.
Needs:
- ❏ index cards
- ❏ pencils
- ❏ string

Before the Study

Before the study, make enough photocopies of the handout on page 25 so that each group of four students can have one. Cut the photocopies in half, separating the "Diagnosis: Leprosy" and "Diagnosis: Sin" sections. Use scissors to cut string into a twenty-four-inch piece for each student.

Warm-Up

Numb-Friends League
(20 to 30 minutes)

After everyone has arrived and settled in,

ASK:

- **Who can tell me some of the symptoms of leprosy?**

Write teenagers' responses on newsprint. If necessary, complete the list by using information from the "Diagnosis: Leprosy" handout (p. 25). Once the list is complete,

SAY:

- **Leprosy isn't that common in our country anymore. But this is one disease that the Bible makes a big deal about. The word *leprosy* or *leper* appears in the Bible over sixty times.**

ASK:

- **Why would the Bible use up so much space talking about leprosy?**

SAY:

- **Today our (rather morbid) goal is to answer the question: What can leprosy teach us about real life today?**

Have students form two teams, and have each team choose one person to act as the "Numb Friend."

SAY:

- **Before we can grasp any lessons from leprosy, we need to understand a bit more about what the disease is like.**

Explain that both teams' goal is to "numbify" their Numb Friends—that is, to insulate their sense of touch so they can't feel anything touch them.

Set out several rolls of toilet paper and tape, and allow teams to go to work. Warn them that the other team will test their work in five minutes, so they need to work fast and do their best.

After five minutes, call time. Stand both Numb Friends in the front of the room, and have them close their eyes. Have teams stand twenty feet away. Give each team member one paper wad, and have teenagers take turns throwing paper wads at the other team's Numb Friend.

Each time either of the Numb Friends feels a paper wad make contact, have that person raise a hand (or make some other gesture to indicate the hit). The team whose Numb Friend has the fewest "hit sensations" at the end of the game wins.

After the game, allow the Numb Friends to remove their numbing material, then have everyone form a circle. Have students form small groups of three or four, and give each group a copy of the "Diagnosis: Leprosy" handout (p. 25). Have groups read the handout and discuss the following questions:

- ■ Imagine that you had leprosy. How would it affect your everyday life?
- ■ What do you think would be the worst thing about living with leprosy? Explain.
- ■ Imagine that doctors discovered a cure for your leprosy, but to be cured you'd have to soak in hot manure for seven days, would you do it? Why or why not?
- ■ What if your leprosy was hidden and had no outward signs, and you were sure the disease wouldn't show symptoms for years to come? Would you still take the cure, or would your pride get in the way? Explain.
- ■ Can you think of other situations in which pride may prevent someone from doing what he or she really needs to do? Share some examples.

SAY:

- ■ Most likely, none of you will ever have to deal with leprosy. But the truth is that all of us suffer from a "disease" that's very much like leprosy in some ways—except this disease attacks the soul instead of the body.

Distribute a copy of the "Diagnosis: Sin" handout (p. 25) to each small group, and invite teenagers to read the handout and compare the similarities between leprosy and sin.

ASK:

- What are some other similarities between leprosy and sin?
- Are these "symptoms" of sin realistic? When have you experienced one of these symptoms in your own life?
- Is there a cure for the disease of sin? Explain.

SAY:

- Our sins separate us from God. We can be cleansed of those sins when we ask God for forgiveness, but our pride often gets in the way. <u>Pride stops the flow of God's forgiveness</u>, the only cure we have for the disease of sin.

The Point ▶

 The term *pride* may be confusing to teenagers because of its many meanings. Pride can keep you from admitting a mistake, or it can inspire you to wear your school colors during football season.

Fortunately, the biblical meaning of *pride* is quite specific. According to the Expository Dictionary of Bible Words (Zondervan), the meaning of *pride* as it's used in Proverbs is simply a "refusal to consider God or respond to him. Instead, the arrogant supposes that human beings can live successfully apart from an obedient relationship with the Lord."

For more verses on pride, see Proverbs 11:2; 13:10; 16:5; 16:18-19; 18:12; 21:4; and 29:23.

Bible Connection: The Price of Pride
(15 to 20 minutes)

SAY:

- We're going to take a deeper look at someone who needed help from God but found that his pride got in the way. As we look at the Scripture today, let's ask God to help us understand this story and how it applies to us personally.

Ask a few young people to voice one-sentence prayers, asking God to help them grasp what the passage is trying to teach them. After the prayers, ask teenagers to form groups of four and read through 2 Kings 5:1-17 together.

SAY:

- Naaman's pride almost kept him from getting the help from God that he needed. That same pride can keep us from God, too, if we let it. Pride stops the flow of forgiveness, but with humility comes healing and life. ◀ **The Point**
- Let's see what we can learn from Naaman's example.

In their small groups, have teenagers discuss each of these questions:

- Why do you think Naaman was so hesitant to wash in the Jordan, even if it meant being healed of leprosy?
- What did Naaman do that reminded you of your own relationship with God? Explain.
- Why do you think we're often so hesitant to go to God or others to ask for forgiveness?
- Based on the information you've heard today, what can the effects of leprosy teach us about the effects of sin in our lives?
- Given all these parallels, why do we still often choose to hang on to sin?

Have a volunteer in each group read aloud Proverbs 3:34. Then have group members discuss these questions:

- This passage says that God resists people who have pride but gives grace to people who are humble. If God really loves us unconditionally, why doesn't he just help us automatically, regardless of our attitude?
- What if you don't think something you do is wrong, even though the Bible says it is? What should you do?

Call everyone together and

SAY:

- Pride happens any time you set aside God's authority in your life and follow your own way instead. Our pride stops the flow of God's forgiveness because it can keep us from coming to God for help. Pride can prevent us from recognizing our *need* for God's forgiveness. Pride has a way of making us believe that we can make it on our own, even though the Bible clearly says that we have no hope outside of Christ.

ASK:
- How does your pride keep you from experiencing God's forgiveness?
- How does your pride keep sin alive in your life?

SAY:
- Letting pride get in the way of your relationship with God costs a heavy price: unforgiveness and a broken relationship.

Bonus Activity

(5 to 10 minutes)

Instead of having groups simply read the Bible passage in 2 Kings 5:1-17, invite them to participate in a creative drama.

Write each of the following character names on separate index cards, then tape or pin a card to the shirt of each young person.

- **Naaman** (commander of Aram's army)
- **Soldiers**
- **Young Servant Girl** (from Israel)
- **Naaman's Wife**
- **Naaman's Master** (king of Aram)
- **The Letter** (sent from the king of Aram to the king of Israel)
- **King of Israel**
- **Elisha, the Man of God**
- **Naaman's Horses and Chariots**
- **Elisha's Messenger**
- **Naaman's Servants**

(Note: If your group is small, it's OK to give teenagers multiple character names. If your group is large, you can make all the extra people Soldiers or Naaman's Servants, or you can form two groups and have each perform the passage in turn.)

Explain that someone will read the passage aloud slowly and allow time for the characters to spontaneously act out their parts.

SAY:
- **As we act our way through this passage, look for things Naaman does that remind you of your relationship with God.**

If you have a highly dramatic reader in your group, ask him or her to read the passage while you participate in the action. Otherwise, read the passage yourself, making sure to pause frequently so teenagers can act out their parts.

Cleansings
(up to 10 minutes)

Life Application

Distribute pencils, strings, and index cards, then have students write their names at one end of their cards.

SAY:

- ■ <u>Pride can stop the flow of forgiveness</u> when it prevents us from truly dealing with our sins. Let's take some time to do that in our own lives.

◀ **The Point**

Give students five minutes to think about and list all the sins they struggle with or may feel ashamed about. Encourage them to think not only about actions, but also about thoughts and inaction. Some students may need more than one card, and that's OK.

When teenagers have finished, have each one use a pencil to punch a small hole in the card and then thread the string through the hole and tie it around his or her ankle.

Explain that the sin we carry around can be a lot like shackles worn by prisoners. Then

SAY:

- ■ I challenge you to not remove your list of sins until you've taken time to talk with God about each item you wrote and ask for his forgiveness. Don't let your pride block the flow of God's forgiveness in your life. Go to him. He's waiting for you.

Invite students to silently pray, then dismiss the class.

FYI: In order to help students honestly evaluate their own sins, give them space during this activity. Encourage students to spread out around the room. When they see that you respect their "comfort zones," they'll come to trust you more.

FYI: Some teenagers may have questions about what it means to ask for God's forgiveness for sins. Tell teenagers that you're available to talk one-on-one at another time, and set up specific meeting times if needed.

▶ Diagnosis: Leprosy

- Leprosy is a slow-growing, chronic infection of the peripheral nervous system. Its initial symptom (often ignored) is numbness in particular areas of the skin.

- With the loss of touch sensation, the body becomes more subject to injury. Without knowing it, a leper can burn, cut, or chafe his or her body with absolutely no sensation of pain.

- For people who have leprosy, the disease becomes the single most dominating factor of their lives.

- When injuries do occur, the natural healing process is hindered because of poor blood circulation to the infected areas. As a result, simple injuries can eventually cause the loss of fingers, toes, nasal tissue, or other parts of the body frequently exposed to the elements.

- Lepers are typically shunned from contact with others.

- As of now, there is still no cure for leprosy.

▶ Diagnosis: Sin

- Sin attacks the soul by slowly "searing" the conscience, taking away its ability to discern right from wrong (1 Timothy 4:1-2). The first sign of this "numbness" (often ignored) is decreased sensitivity to sin.

- With the loss of spiritual sensitivity, the soul becomes more subject to injury. Without realizing it, a person's continued sin can undermine his or her sense of purpose and destroy vital relationships (Ephesians 4:17-19).

- People who continue to sin become enslaved to it (Romans 6:15-23).

- When sinful actions do injure a person's heart, the healing process is hindered or halted altogether because the sin separates the person from God (Isaiah 59:1-2). Hurts that are kept from God will eventually result in complete emotional and spiritual deadness.

- Sin creates a barrier to intimacy between people (Galatians 5:13-15).

- Jesus provided the cure for sin at the cost of his own life (1 Peter 2:24).

Permission to photocopy this handout from Faith 4 Life: Junior High Bible Study Series, *Becoming a Christian* granted for local church use.
Copyright © Group Publishing, Inc., P.O. Box 481, Loveland, CO 80539. www.grouppublishing.com

The Case of the Empty Tomb

Study 3

Death. When you're young, you usually don't think about it. Why should you? You have your whole life ahead of you.

And then it's in the news—the drive-by shooting of a thirteen-year-old boy; the kidnapping and murder of an eleven-year-old girl; the senseless, drunken-driving collision extinguishing the lives of an entire family.

All of a sudden, death doesn't seem so far away.

And then the questions arise. Where do we go when we die? Is death just a big, black void? Or is there something more?

Your teenagers ask these questions—they need answers.

Your young people need to know that Jesus beat death so they wouldn't have to face it. Jesus rose from the grave to give them what they can't get anywhere else: forgiveness and eternal life.

In this study, teenagers will debate whether Jesus really rose from the dead from the perspectives of the Pharisees, the Romans, and the disciples. Through this debate, teenagers will discover the only possible explanation for Jesus' disappearance from the grave: He's alive!

The Point

▶ Jesus rose from the dead so we can be forgiven.

Scripture Source

Psalm 49:15; Isaiah 53:12

These passages prophesy Jesus' death and resurrection.

Various Gospel passages

These passages describe Jesus' arrest, trial, death, burial, resurrection, and post-resurrection appearances.

John 11:25

John writes about Jesus' promise of new life.

Romans 6:23; 10:9-13

Paul explains the relationship between faith in Jesus' resurrection and forgiveness of sins.

The Study at a Glance

Warm-Up (up to 5 minutes)

Bait the Debate

What students will do: Prepare to debate whether Jesus rose from the dead.

Needs: ❑ paper towels
❑ index cards

Bible Connection (35-45 minutes)

Making the Case

Round 1

What students will do: Debate whether someone stole Jesus' body.

Needs: ❑ Bibles
❑ "Round 1 Cards" handout (p. 34)
❑ pencils

Round 2

What students will do: Debate whether Jesus was buried alive.

Needs: ❑ Bibles
❑ "Round 2 Cards" handout (p. 35)

Round 3

What students will do: Debate whether the Romans crucified the wrong man or an impostor appeared to Jesus' followers.

Needs: ❑ Bibles
❑ "Round 3 Cards" handout (p. 36)

Life Application (5-10 minutes)

Material Prayer

What students will do: Create prayers from supplies used in the study.

Needs: ❑ Bibles

Before the Study →

Before the study begins, photocopy "Round 1 Cards," "Round 2 Cards," and "Round 3 Cards" (pp. 34-36), and cut the copies along the dashed lines. Arrange the round cards by group—Pharisees, Romans, and Disciples—and in numerical order.

Gather enough index cards for each student to have one. Arrange the cards in three equal piles. Label each card in one pile "Pharisees," each card in another pile "Romans," and each card in the third pile "Disciples."

For each student, tear off a three-square strip from a roll of paper towels.

Warm-Up

Bait the Debate
(up to 5 minutes)

As students arrive, hand each one a strip of paper towels and an index card labeled "Pharisees," "Romans," or "Disciples." Keep the three groups as even in number as possible. Have the Pharisees drape their paper towels over their heads to represent prayer shawls. Have the Romans wear their paper towels as capes, tucking one end of the towel strips into the backs of their shirt collars. Have the Disciples tuck their paper towels into the waists of their pants, representing the loincloths of servants and reflecting their positions as God's servants.

SAY:

- You're all here to solve a mystery.
- A few weeks ago, Jesus of Nazareth was arrested, beaten, and nailed to a cross. He supposedly died and was buried in a tomb carved from solid stone. The tomb's only entrance was blocked by a large rock, sealed, and placed under Roman guard.
- But now the body is missing. Some say Jesus rose from the dead; others deny this possibility. Pontius Pilate demands to know where the body is and how it got past the guards.
- To get to the bottom of this mystery, all of you—Pharisees, Romans, and Disciples—will debate the possible reasons for Jesus' disappearance. We'll have three rounds of discussion. For each round, I'll give your group a round card that outlines your group's strategy for explaining the disappearance of Jesus' body. Look up the Bible verses, and take notes on your index card. Who knows? Perhaps we'll discover that Jesus really rose from the dead.

The Point ▶

Making the Case
(35 to 45 minutes)

Round 1

Give groups pencils, and send them to three different corners of the room—one corner for Pharisees, one for Romans, and one for Disciples. Have teenagers form pairs within their groups.

SAY:

- During each round of debate, each group will choose one pair to argue the group's case. The person with a birthday closest to today and his or her partner will go first. That pair will go to the front of the room and, within thirty seconds, state the group's opening arguments. After all three opening arguments, any pair may make a statement. But every pair in your group must have one turn at the front of the room before any pair takes a second turn.

Hand each group its "Round 1 Card," and

SAY:

- Rumor has it that Jesus' body was stolen from the grave. Study your round cards and the verses listed on them to prepare your arguments for this round.

After five minutes, call the groups together and

ASK:

- Does anyone have something to say about the disappearance of Jesus' body?

Have each group send one pair to the front of the room for opening arguments, and allow one pair to volunteer to begin the debate. Allow teenagers to debate for five minutes, including opening arguments.

Then have pairs discuss these questions:

- Would stealing Jesus' body help your group? Why or why not?
- At this point in the debate, do you think any of the three groups has taken Jesus' body? If so, who and why?
- What might be other explanations for the empty tomb?
- What's your reaction to being a (Pharisee, Roman, Disciple)?
- How do you think the other groups feel?

Bible Connection

FYI

At the beginning of each round, have groups choose a pair to send to the front of the room. Make sure groups choose pairs that haven't spoken in front of the group yet. If all pairs have had a turn, allow pairs to volunteer for the task.

The Point ▶

SAY:

■ Did someone take the body from the tomb? Or could it be that <u>Jesus really rose from the dead</u>? We'll find out more in Round 2.

Round 2

SAY:

■ Somebody may or may not have stolen Jesus' body from the tomb. Or maybe Jesus wasn't really dead when he was buried.

Give groups their "Round 2 Cards," and allow them five minutes to study their verses and develop their arguments.

Have each group send one pair to the front of the room for opening arguments. Allow groups to refute each other's statements. Five minutes after opening arguments begin, have teenagers return to their pairs to discuss these questions:

■ Do you think Jesus fainted and was buried alive? Why or why not?
■ What are other possible explanations for the empty tomb?
■ What's your reaction to being a (Pharisee, Roman, Disciple) now?
■ How do you think the other groups feel?

SAY:

■ So far, we've discussed whether someone stole Jesus' body and whether Jesus really wasn't dead when he was buried. We may discover that <u>Jesus really rose from the dead</u>. But before we conclude that, we have one more round of debate.

The Point ▶

Round 3

SAY:

■ In this next round, we'll find out if Jesus really was killed. Maybe the Romans killed the wrong guy!

Give groups their "Round 3 Cards," and allow five minutes to study the verses and develop arguments.

Have each group send one pair to the front of the room for opening arguments, and allow one pair to begin the round. After five minutes

> **FYI**
> During each round of debate, keep an eye on your copy of the round cards. If there is a lull in the conversation, you can generate debate by mentioning something on one of the cards that no one has said yet. For example, during Round 1 you could say, "The Pharisees mentioned something to me earlier about a meeting they had after Jesus' body was discovered missing. Does anybody know about that?"

of opening arguments and debate, have teenagers return to their pairs to discuss these questions:

- Do you think the sightings of Jesus were a case of mistaken identity? Explain.
- What's your reaction to being a (Pharisee, Roman, Disciple)?
- How do you think the other groups feel?
- Which group do you wish you could have been in? Why?
- Based on all the information you now have, could Jesus have risen from the dead? Why or why not?
- What would it mean to you if Jesus did rise from the dead? Explain.

SAY:

- Since we can't prove that anyone took Jesus' body or faked his resurrection, perhaps we should conclude that <u>Jesus Christ really rose from the dead</u>. ◀ **The Point**

Material Prayer
(5 to 10 minutes)

Life Application

SAY:

- Jesus rose from the dead, but what does that mean to you and me? And what does that have to do with the sin that separates us from God? As we close today, we'll discover how important Jesus' resurrection is to us. <u>Jesus rose from the dead so we can be forgiven</u>. ◀ **The Point**

Have teenagers form trios composed of one person from each debate group. Have trios read Romans 6:23; 10:9-13 and consider how faith in Jesus' death and resurrection relates to salvation. Invite them to think about these questions and use them to kick-start their discussion:

- How does it make you feel to know that Jesus paid the penalty for sin by dying on the cross?
- How do Jesus' death and resurrection affect you personally? How do they impact your relationship with God?
- Do you personally believe that Jesus died for your sins? Why or why not?

32

Some teenagers may have questions about Jesus' death and resurrection and what that means to them. Tell teenagers that you're available to talk with them individually to help them process their questions.

Have trios create a "material prayer." Have trios use materials in the room, such as paper towels, chairs, or pencils, to create a visual prayer. For example, they could wrap a pencil in paper towels and then unravel it as they thank Jesus for dying and rising from the grave for them.

Have trio members share with each other how they'll respond this week to Jesus' resurrection. For example, teenagers may decide to make a decision to put their faith in Jesus. Others may decide to explain Jesus' resurrection to a friend from school.

Pharisees

ROUND 1

You Pharisees are well-educated, important teachers who people respect and ask for guidance. You never liked Jesus. He challenged and insulted you in front of your followers, and then he did all those miracles and gained his own following. He was dangerous.

So you had Jesus arrested and set it up so the Romans killed him. But now his body is missing. Jesus predicted he'd rise from the dead; his disciples may claim Jesus' disappearance as proof that he was the Messiah. Bad news.

Your Strategy

1. Read Matthew 28:1-4, 11-15. What happened in the cemetery? How did you and the Romans decide to handle it?

2. Accuse the Disciples of stealing Jesus' body. The Disciples believed Jesus would rise from the dead; they probably took the body to make it appear that he did.

3. If accusing the Disciples doesn't work, blame the Romans. You pushed them into killing Jesus; maybe they're paying you back by making life hard for you.

4. If you're accused, mention your religious laws that forbid touching dead bodies—laws you'd never break.

Romans

ROUND 1

The Roman Legion is one of the world's greatest armies. You're tough, and you don't make mistakes following orders.

Pilate commissioned you to guard Jesus' tomb, and because Jesus' crucifixion was political, you took special care standing guard. But now the body is gone. It looks bad for you because Roman soldiers who fail to follow orders are often executed.

Your Strategy

1. Read Matthew 27:57-66. Use the information in this passage to argue that you did what you were told. Did Pilate send you to guard the right tomb? Who secured the tomb—you or the Pharisees?

2. Accuse the Pharisees of not securing the tomb. If the tomb wasn't properly secured, anyone could have stolen the body.

3. Accuse the Pharisees of taking the body to cause a riot.

4. Read Matthew 28:1-4, 11-15 to protect yourself. What happened in the cemetery? How did you and the Pharisees decide to handle it? You'll be in trouble if word of what happened reaches your commander, so don't admit it. Team up with the Pharisees to cover your tracks.

Disciples

ROUND 1

A few days ago, your world collapsed—Jesus was dead. You saw it all, from his arrest to his burial. Only John was brave enough to be out front; but you hung in the shadows. And there were hundreds of other witnesses.

Then the women dragged you out to the cemetery, where the stone was rolled away and Jesus' tomb was empty! And later you were in the room when he appeared. So you know—he's alive again!

Your Strategy

1. Read John 20:1-29 to review what you've been through lately: Mary Magdalene reported someone had taken Jesus' body, Peter and John checked out the tomb, Mary saw Jesus alive, then all of you saw Jesus.

2. If you're accused of stealing Jesus' body, say that you were too afraid to try it. You fled the scene earlier and were hiding out. And why would you take the body? His death surprised you, too. Besides, how could you sneak through a heavily armed Roman guard?

3. Even if the Romans and Pharisees blame each other and you for stealing Jesus' body, accuse no one. Why? Because you know the truth—he's alive!

4. Read Psalm 49:15 and Isaiah 53:12 to discover prophecies about Jesus' death and resurrection. Match the information in these verses with the facts of Jesus' death to argue that Jesus is alive.

Permission to photocopy this handout from Faith 4 Life: Junior High Bible Study Series, *Becoming a Christian* granted for local church use. Copyright © Group Publishing, Inc., P.O. Box 481, Loveland, CO 80539. www.grouppublishing.com

Pharisees

1. Check the events, and collect your ammo for blaming the Romans. Read John 19:31-33, and answer these questions: Of the men they crucified, who died first? Why didn't the Romans break Jesus' legs? Could this be the cover-up you hoped to find? If no one stole Jesus' body, he must have been alive when sealed in the tomb. Maybe Jesus just passed out because of the pain.

2. Blame Pilate—after all, he's one of those Romans! Read John 18:38-40, and review what Pilate wanted to do with Jesus. Pilate didn't want to crucify Jesus; he offered Barabbas as a substitute. Maybe he set this up!

Romans

1. Read Mark 15:37-41 to review whether you were present at Jesus' death and who else saw Jesus die. If you're accused of burying Jesus alive, mention all the people who knew that Jesus was dead.

2. Read Luke 23:44-49 and John 19:31-37 to review how you knew Jesus was dead. If you're accused, mention this evidence that Jesus really was dead.

Disciples

1. Read Luke 23:50-54 and John 19:38-42 to review how the men prepared Jesus' body for burial. They wrapped him in strips of cloth sprinkled with a mixture of myrrh and aloe. As an honor to Jesus, they prepared his body with more of these spices than usual—almost seventy-five pounds! The men also covered his face with a separate cloth. Remind the Pharisees and Romans of these details of Jesus' burial; if Jesus had been alive, he couldn't have seen or moved wrapped in all those cloths and spices.

2. Also remind the Pharisees and Romans that Jesus' body was trapped behind a stone estimated to weigh at least a ton. The strongest person in the world couldn't have gotten out of that cave and overpowered the guards, let alone a wounded man taken for dead by dozens of witnesses.

Permission to photocopy this handout from Faith 4 Life: Junior High Bible Study Series, *Becoming a Christian* granted for local church use. Copyright © Group Publishing, Inc., P.O. Box 481, Loveland, CO 80539. www.grouppublishing.com

Pharisees

ROUND 3

1. The Romans will probably claim you sent them the wrong man, but why would you? You wanted Jesus dead too. Read the following passages to discover who else identified the man you accused as Jesus: Matthew 26:47-49, 55-57; 27:22-24; John 19:26-27.

2. Suggest that the Disciples are confused about seeing Jesus after his death. They're emotionally unstable, upset, and not to be trusted. Or maybe they've seen a ghost. Say so.

Romans

ROUND 3

1. If the Disciples have seen Jesus, the Pharisees must have sent you the wrong guy to kill. Say so. Loudly.

2. Maybe the Disciples are wrong. They say they've spotted Jesus, but everyone in a robe looks pretty much the same from a distance and in bad light. They've probably just seen a ghost!

Disciples

ROUND 3

1. If anyone says you're wrong about seeing Jesus, be ready. Jesus hasn't appeared as a ghost floating in vapor. He's alive again—in his body!

2. Look up the following passages. Note the time of day Jesus appeared (if it's mentioned), who saw him, and if there's any evidence he's a very real physical being: Matthew 28:1-10; Luke 24:13-16, 28-31, 36-43; John 20:26-31; 21:1-13; 1 Corinthians 15:6-7.

Permission to photocopy this handout from Faith 4 Life: Junior High Bible Study Series, *Becoming a Christian* granted for local church use. Copyright © Group Publishing, Inc., P.O. Box 481, Loveland, CO 80539. www.grouppublishing.com

Study 4

Face the Light

Teenagers live in a world that glorifies human endeavor and achievement. By the time they finish elementary school, most children have learned to tout their strengths and hide their weaknesses in order to be accepted and admired. By watching others cover up their mistakes, it's easy for teenagers to come to the conclusion that admirable people either don't make mistakes or don't get caught making them.

But refusal to admit our mistakes distances us from God. It trivializes sin, and it leads to doubts about our relationship and standing before God. Romans 3:23-24 explains that "all have sinned and fall short of the glory of God, and are justified freely by his grace through the redemption that came by Christ Jesus." Repentance brings restoration. Only by turning from our sin and turning toward the salvation of Jesus can we be changed.

The Point

▶ Admitting you're wrong helps you experience God's forgiveness.

Scripture Source

Psalm 103:8-12; Isaiah 1:18; Mark 2:17

These passages assure us of God's forgiveness.

Isaiah 53:4-6; Romans 4:25–5:1

These passages refer to Jesus' death and resurrection.

Luke 15:8-10; 2 Corinthians 7:10-11; 1 John 1:8-10

These passages show how sin should be dealt with.

Hebrews 4:13

This verse explains that God is omniscient.

The Study at a Glance

Warm-Up (up to 10 minutes)

Cup-to-Cup Relay

What students will do: Participate in a race and see that making mistakes in life is inevitable.

Needs:
- ❏ bucket
- ❏ warm water
- ❏ measuring spoons
- ❏ laundry detergent
- ❏ white vinegar
- ❏ old bedsheet
- ❏ fruit juice
- ❏ paper cups
- ❏ table

Bonus Activity (5-10 minutes)

What students will do: Search for "hidden" images and compare the activity to detecting sin in our lives.

Needs: ❏ Magic Eye 3-D pictures

Bible Connection (25-35 minutes)

Treasure Hunt

What students will do: Use clues to search for a hidden treasure and analyze Bible verses that describe humanity's need for—and God's response to—true repentance.

Needs:
- ❏ Bibles
- ❏ "Clues" handouts (p. 45)
- ❏ "Mistake Tokens" handouts (p. 46)
- ❏ scissors
- ❏ tape
- ❏ bag
- ❏ cupcakes or cookies
- ❏ pencils
- ❏ paper

Life Application (10-15 minutes)

List 'Em and Leave 'Em

What students will do: Recall and ask forgiveness for past mistakes and tear up reminders of their sins.

Needs:
- ❏ Bible
- ❏ pencils
- ❏ Mistake Tokens from "Treasure Hunt" activity
- ❏ bedsheet from "Cup-to-Cup Relay" activity

Before the Study →

Before the study, for the "Cup-to-Cup Relay" activity, mix a stain-removal solution of one quart warm water, one teaspoon laundry detergent, and one tablespoon white vinegar in a bucket. Also drape a white bedsheet over a table.

For the "Treasure Hunt" activity, think of clues that will lead your teenagers to specific areas of your building or the surrounding area. The first clue should lead teenagers to the second clue. The second clue should lead teenagers to the third clue, and so forth. Write the clues in the spaces provided on the "Clues" handout (p. 45), and make one copy for every two teenagers in your class. Cut the clues into separate strips, and tape one copy each of Clue #2 through Clue #5 in the area described by the previous clue. For example, if Clue #1 leads teenagers to the drinking fountain, make certain Clue #2 is hidden near the fountain. Keep the remainder of the clue copies for later use. Bake or buy enough cupcakes or cookies for everyone in your class. Place two of these treats in a small bag, tape one copy of Clue #6 to the bag, and hide the treats. For every two teenagers in your class, make one copy of the "Mistake Tokens" handout (p. 46), and cut out the tokens. Store the rest of the treats where teenagers won't discover them.

Warm-Up

Cup-to-Cup Relay
(up to 10 minutes)

FYI: Create clues that will send teenagers in different directions throughout the area. For example, if you have more than one exit sign in your building, create a clue that will lead teenagers to the signs.

After teenagers arrive, explain that this lesson is about turning to God, trusting in Jesus' death and resurrection, and asking for forgiveness of our sins. Have the class form two teams, and ask them to stand on opposite sides of a table and face each other. Give each player a paper cup. Pour juice into the cups of the two opposing players at one end of the table. Join one of the teams, and explain that when you say "go," the first person on each team will pour the juice from his or her cup into the next person's cup. That person will pour the juice into the next person's cup, and so on, until the juice has been poured from cup to cup all the way down the line and back again.

Explain that the goal is for one team to finish the relay first with the most juice left in the last cup. Remind teenagers to do their pouring over the sheet and to pour as fast as they can. If the teenagers don't spill a drop of juice onto the sheet, make certain you do.

When the game is over,

SAY:

- We've all made messes in the past. None of us is perfect, and we all sin. Imagine for a moment that this sheet represents your life and the stains are the sins you've committed.

ASK:

- In what way are the sins you've committed like these stains?
- How are they different?
- If you were looking at your life through God's eyes, would it have more stains or fewer stains than this sheet?
- Would the amount of stains matter in God's eyes? Explain.

SAY:

- We've *all* made choices or had thoughts that are sinful—that separate us from God. Some of the sins we commit are very visible, like these stains. Other sins are not easily seen—either we're good at hiding them or we don't know that we aren't even aware of them. Sometimes sin can be hard to detect. But it's important for us to recognize our sin because <u>admitting you're wrong helps you experience God's forgiveness</u>. ◀ **The Point**

Immerse the sheet in the bucket of stain-removal solution you made before the study, and let it soak while you proceed with the rest of the lesson.

> **FYI**
>
> Before the "Cup-to-Cup Relay," test the bedsheet material and the juice brand you plan to use to make certain the stain-removal solution will work. The solution does work with cotton sheets and bottled Libby Juicy, 100 Percent Fruit Juice (apple and grape juice mix), and ShurFine frozen Cranberry-Raspberry Juice Cocktail.

Bonus Activity

(5 to 10 minutes)

If you have time, try this discussion starter after the "Cup-to-Cup Relay."

For this activity, you'll need to find some Magic Eye illusions. Three-dimensional Magic Eye illusions are distributed by Universal Press Syndicate and appear in many newspapers' Sunday comics. Many bookstores and libraries also carry Magic Eye books. More information about Magic Eye pictures can be found at www.magiceye.com.

Pass the Magic Eye pictures around, and explain the following techniques for seeing the hidden images:

- Hold the picture close to your face, relax your eyes, and focus on a point "beyond" the picture. Slowly move the picture away from your face, and keep staring "through" it until the 3-D image becomes apparent.

- If the Magic Eye picture is printed on glossy paper, hold it so that you can see an object being reflected. Fix your gaze on the object until you see depth in the Magic Eye picture.

Give teenagers a few minutes to try to find the hidden images.

After everyone has had a chance to search for a 3-D image, ask teenagers whether they thought this activity was easy or difficult.

SAY:

- Sometimes our sins are not as visible as stains on a sheet. For human beings, seeing the sin in our own lives can be like trying to find the 3-D images in these pictures. Let's hear what the Bible has to say about *God's* ability to see sin.

Ask a volunteer to read aloud Hebrews 4:13.

ASK:

- What kinds of sins are difficult for us to see? easy for us to see?
- What does our society say we should do about our sins? Explain.
- How does it feel to apologize to people? to God?
- How does it feel to have someone apologize to you when that person isn't really sorry for what he or she has done?
- Do we have to be sorry for our sins to be forgiven by God? Explain.

SAY:

- No matter how good we try to be, we're *all* guilty of sin. God wants us to be genuinely sorry for the mistakes we've made. When we repent and put our trust in Jesus, God forgives us. In fact, God says he will forget our sins as if they never happened! His forgiveness brings true healing and genuine change. It's amazing and wonderful how admitting you're wrong and accepting Jesus' forgiveness helps you change your ways.

Bible Connection: Treasure Hunt

(25 to 35 minutes)

Have teenagers form pairs. Give each pair a Bible and a pencil.

SAY:

- You and your partner are going to go on a treasure hunt by following clues. I'll give you the first clue that will lead to the second clue. If your pair finds the second clue, remove it, look up the Bible verse on it, write down the answer to the question, and search for the third clue. You must answer the question before moving on to the next clue.

- If your pair finds a clue, don't return it for others to use. The teams who don't find a clue must come to me to receive the clue and a Mistake Token. Even if you get the clue from me, you must look up the Bible verse and write down the answer to the question before you move on. Continue searching for clues until the treasure is found.

Tell teenagers that partners must stay together and that talking between pairs is not allowed. Once the treasure has been found, have teenagers come back together. If the treasure has not been found after fifteen minutes, have teenagers come back together, give a copy of Clue #5 to all the pairs and then let them search. Ask the winning pair to show the treasure to the rest of the class and consume the treasure. Then surprise everyone by providing treats for the rest of the class.

While teenagers enjoy their snacks, have each pair share one answer to the questions under the clues. Then ask:

- Was it difficult to know when to come to me for help?
- How did you feel when I gave you a Mistake Token?
- What happened if you waited a long time to admit you were on the wrong track?
- How did you feel when you heard or saw other teams find the clues before you did?
- Why do you think it's difficult for us to admit when we're wrong?
- What was the main message of the Bible verses you read? Explain them in your own words.
- Which of the Bible verses you read meant the most to you? Why?

> **FYI:** If you have an opportunity to use a large area for this activity, provide boundaries so your teenagers don't wander too far away from your meeting area.

> **FYI:** If the lesson must be conducted within a confined area, teenagers can play a written version of the game. To do this, have teenagers guess the imaginary location of each clue until they "find" the treasure. Teams can guess as many times as they want (submitting their answers on pieces of paper) but should receive a Mistake Token for every incorrect guess. When a team guesses correctly, the leader should give that team the next clue.

- Why do you think repentance is so important to God?
- How do you feel about what Jesus did on the cross to pay the penalty for your sins?

SAY:

The Point ▶

- Because of what Jesus did on the cross, we can have peace with God. <u>Admitting you're wrong helps you experience God's forgiveness</u> and gives you a new start! God will help you change your ways. Repentance is the first step to true change and growth. When we're too proud to come to God for his help, we force ourselves to continue in damaging behavior. When we let go of our pride and admit our errors, we give God the opportunity to begin the process of change in our hearts and to point us in the right direction.

Life Application

List 'Em and Leave 'Em
(10 to 15 minutes)

Have teenagers redistribute their Mistake Tokens so that every person has one. Then have everyone spread out and write on the back of the tokens things they're sorry they've done or neglected to do. After a few minutes, have a volunteer read aloud Psalm 103:8-12.

ASK:

- How should our sins be punished?
- Do you see God as forgiving or judging? Why?
- Is it ever difficult for you to believe that when you've confessed your sins, they have been removed as far as the east is from the west? Explain.

Lift the bedsheet that has been soaking in the stain-removal solution, and show it to the class.

SAY:

- Remember how soiled this was after we played the first game? Every time someone goofed and spilled some juice, it left a stain. In the same way, our sins cause spiritual stains. When we sin, sometimes we can make amends and sometimes we can't. But because of Jesus' love for us, he died on the cross and took our punishment for our sins, then rose from the dead three days later. He offers us a chance at a new start, stain-free! When we admit that we have sinned and have faith in Jesus' death and resurrection, God promises to forgive us and help us start over.

Ask a volunteer to read aloud Isaiah 1:18.

Have teenagers return to their pairs from the "Treasure Hunt" activity and then spread out around the room. Encourage teenagers to ask God for forgiveness for the sins written on their tokens. Explain that if they feel comfortable doing so, they can confess their sins to their partners and pray together, or they can choose to confess and pray silently. When teenagers finish praying, have them stand up, tear their tokens into pieces, and throw them in the air. Have partners remind each other that their sins have been forgiven.

PRAY:

■ **Jesus, thank you for being a merciful God who does not hold grudges. Thank you for not expecting us to be perfect and for being so patient with us. Thank you for taking the punishment for our sins and dying on the cross because of your love for us. We're sorry for these sins in our lives. Thank you for removing them from us as far as the east is from the west. Help us to <u>admit when we're wrong so that we can experience your forgiveness</u>. In Jesus' name, amen.**

◀ **The Point**

Thank teenagers for coming to class, and tell them to leave their sins behind.

> **FYI**
>
> As you lift the bedsheet out of the stain-removal solution, be careful not to allow the water to stain your carpet.

Clue #1

_____

_____

Read Mark 2:17 • How is sin like a sickness? _____

_____

Clue #2

_____

_____

Read Isaiah 53:4-6 • What happened to Jesus because of our sins? _____

_____

Clue #3

_____

_____

Read Romans 4:25—5:1 • What did Jesus' death accomplish? _____

_____

Clue #4

_____

_____

Read 1 John 1:8-10 • Why do we have to repent of our sins? _____

_____

Clue #5

_____

_____

Read 2 Corinthians 7:10-11 • What changes does repentance bring about?

_____

Clue #6

_____

_____

Read Luke 15:8-10 • Why do you think angels are glad when sinners repent?

_____

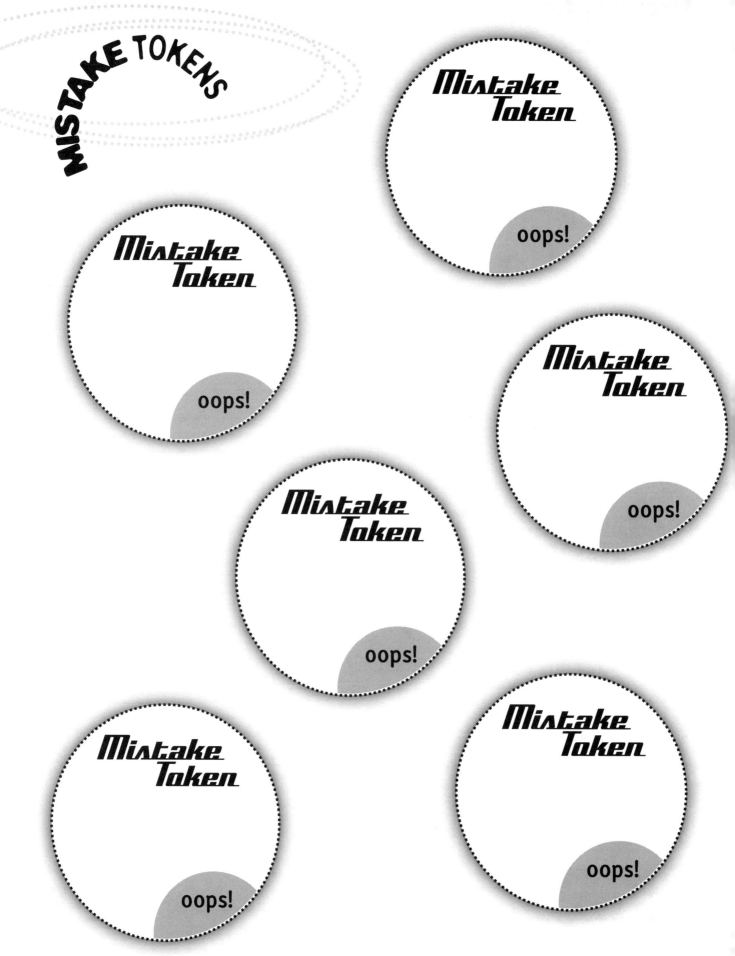

Changed 4 Life

To get an idea of what your students have learned during your study of *Becoming a Christian*, make a note on your calendar four weeks from now and plan to dedicate some time to discussing the following questions with your students:

ASK:

- **What do you remember most about our study about becoming a Christian? Why?**

- **How have you applied what you learned to your life?**

Invite students to form pairs and practice summarizing, in their own words, what it means to become a Christian. Encourage them to include a bit of their own faith story in their explanation.

becoming a christian

Look for the Whole Family of Faith 4 Life Bible Studies!

Senior High Books
- Family Matters
- Is There Life After High School?
- Prayer
- Sharing Your Faith

Junior High Books
- Becoming a Christian
- Finding Your Identity
- God's Purpose for Me
- Understanding the Bible

Preteen Books
- Being Responsible
- Getting Along With Others
- God in My Life
- Going Through Tough Times

Coming Soon!

for Senior High
- Applying God's Word
- Christian Character
- Sexuality
- Your Christian ID
- Believing in Jesus
- Following Jesus
- Worshipping 24/7
- Your Relationships

for Junior High
- Choosing Wisely
- Friends
- My Family Life
- Sharing Jesus
- Fighting Temptation
- How to Pray
- My Life as a Christian
- Who Is God?

for Preteens
- Building Friendships
- How to Make Great Choices
- Succeeding in School
- What's a Christian?
- Handling Conflict
- Peer Pressure
- The Bible and Me
- Why God Made Me

Visit your local Christian bookstore,
or contact Group Publishing, Inc., at 800-447-1070.
www.grouppublishing.com